Coming Clean

Also by Tom Gunn:

GunnSights: Taking Aim on Selling in the High-Stakes Industry of International Aerospace   Naval Institute Press, 2008.

Coming Clean

TOM GUNN

A Handbook

Copyright © 2010, Tom Gunn

Library of Congress Cataloging-in-Publication Data

Gunn, Thomas, 1943–
    Coming Clean: A Handbook
        p. cm.
    ISBN / 1453705929 (softcover)
    EAN-13 / 9781453705926
    1. Alcoholics Anonymous 2. Alcoholics—
Rehabilitation 3. Recovering Alcoholics—Services for
4. Drug Addiction 5. Twelve Step Programs
    I. Title

DEDICATION

To my brother Jim. He brought me in, saved my life and taught me to accept life on life's terms.

And to Kate, love of my life, for her loyalty, understanding, and support.

CONTENTS

Preface / **1**

My Story / **9**

Transition / **23**

Everybody Drinks / **41**

    Self-Help **45**

    Where to Start **46**

    Counseling **48**

    Pharmacotherapy **50**

    Psychotherapy **51**

Alcoholics Anonymous / **53**

    The Meeting **55**

    To Find a Meeting **59**

    On the Ground **61**

    Comes the Hard Part **63**

    Sponsors **65**

    The Twelve Steps / **69**

My Story . . . and Others / **93**

Lessons Learned and Shared / **113**

Epilog / **117**

PREFACE

If you think you have a drinking problem, you probably do. If you think you can handle it without any outside help, you're probably wrong. In fact, I'll bet you've tried. And still have a problem.

Let me guess . . . you've tested AA, or at least sort of. You went on the internet (ah, that blessed anonymity, no need to actually ask a *person)* and found the location of a meeting. Probably on the other side of town or even in the next town, you certainly didn't want to run into anyone you actually knew. You drove to the spot and parked in the most remote part of the lot. And sat in your car, watching the people arrive. Young or old, well-dressed businessmen on the way home from the office or farmers just in from the field or—was that Louie from the garage? Did that guy look like your dentist? Nah, strangers all. Good.

But you didn't go in, it didn't feel, well, *right.* And you stopped in at that friendly-looking bar you spotted back up the road to prove to yourself that you didn't really need AA.

Or, maybe you actually went to meetings, perhaps not all the same one, spread it around, because, well, you really didn't want to become *involved,* you just wanted cover to continue drinking so your wife (or husband or significant other or domestic partner) would get off your back. "Honey," you'd say with a touch of pride, "I'm working on it, going to AA meetings." Probably didn't fool whoever for long and when he/she/them finally walked out, maybe you found this book. On the internet, of course. Sent discreetly to your home in a plain brown wrapper, no need to expose your anxieties to a librarian or bookstore clerk. Or, just maybe, someone at work, some "well-meaning friend," handed you a copy as a gentle hint.

"So," I hear you asking, "what do I do now, coach?"

In more than twenty-five years of sobriety, I've talked with thousands of users and abusers. All have a story. Each thinks theirs is unique. They became an alcoholic *because.*

☐ "I have childhood memories (or nightmares) of a father drunk at dinner every night, finding fault (my grades were never good enough), fighting with my mother (the soup was cold, he couldn't find a clean shirt, can she ever do anything right?). No wonder I took to alcohol." So . . . it was someone else's fault?

☐ Or, "I started drinking *because* of a failed romance in the 12th grade, bad acne, a "D" in Latin—all hitting at the same time. Who wouldn't take to booze?" Wrong. A lot of people who suffer through all-of-the-above may drink a lot but don't become alcoholics.

☐ Or, *"Because* of all that mandatory fraternity/sorority partying in college, every weekend, before the game, during the game, after the game. So much *fun."* And oh, by the way, "it was my first time living away from home, I was hormone-challenged and had to deal with so many temptations thrown in my path." I hope you had responsible fun, but a lot people drank too much in college, played around, and didn't end up alcoholic.

☐ Or, "*Because* I'm kinda shy and insecure and drinking helps me loosen up, open up, talk with strangers." It's not surprising that alcohol has been called the "social lubricant." But a lot of people drink to overcome inhibitions and dampen anxiety and don't become alcoholics.

☐ Or, "My job, the pressure . . . [I'm a judge] [I'm a doctor] I make life-and-death decisions every day" or, "I'm a [fireman] [police officer] [military professional] and face death every day," or, "I'm a [teacher] [lawyer] [priest] under great pressure, dealing with unruly kids or other folk's problems all day, can't wait to get home and relax," or "I'm a salesman and unless your job depends on making the next big sale, you simply can't understand . . ."

You get the idea. Every alcoholic has a story. Each thinks their excuse is unique.

But a lot of people, maybe most, drink because they like to take a drink or two for no particular reason, watching the TV news after work, having dinner, partying with friends. Just so, a lot of alcoholics start out drinking for no particular reason, no *because*. Unless . . . they reach a point where they *need* to drink and can't stop drinking once they've begun. One more for the road . . .

And that's the key. It doesn't make much difference *why* you started drinking in the first place, back in the dim and distant past. Understand, right up front: the American Medical Association affirms that alcoholism is a disease, maybe planted in the genes, some chemical imbalance in your brain.

And there is no cure.

You are not alone; perhaps one-in-ten adult Americans, maybe eighteen million of us are alcoholics (or serious alcohol abusers), about two-thirds are men, one-third, women.

However . . . let me step back for a moment. Perhaps your problem has nothing to do with alcohol—you're imprisoned by drugs, or gambling or sex—and you feel excluded from the discussion by all of this talk about drinking. If you wish, mentally substitute "addiction" every time I write "alcoholism." To me, the terms are pretty much interchangeable because I was for many years a dual-abuser of alcohol and pills.

So, to help you feel at ease . . . I'll bring you into the picture. Let's say, you broke something skiing or were in an auto accident or suffered through major but life-saving surgery. You were in great pain and got blessed relief from some chemical: Demerol, Vicodin, Percodan, Percoset, Oxycontin.

However, long after the pain was gone the pills gave you so much continued pleasure—oh, floating on a cloud or euphoria or standing tall— and you probably had to increase the dosage as you became habituated. Probably became harder and harder to get a regular supply—you can fool your doctor for only so long, and after a while you start to run out of doctors. Or, when the pharmacist punches in your name, the narcotics registry catches up with you; didn't you just fill a prescription yesterday at another drugstore?

But you don't have a *problem,* you just want to be prepared, the pain might come back and a taking a pill or two every now and then might prevent a relapse. Rather like hanging a bag of garlic around your neck to ward off vampires.

You might suspect that you do have a problem when you start looking into the medicine cabinets of friends and family and you *know* you have a problem when you start pinching off a few pills, or a dozen, from each. After all, there were almost ninety in the bottle, who is going to notice? And if you have a dozen or two dozen close friends you can set up a self-directed supply system. And then . . . you *really* know that you have a problem when you start re-connecting with long-ago friends from high school who had recent accidents or surgery. You're bound to strike it rich every once in a while.

If any of this sounds familiar . . . keep reading.

Your story? Sure, I'd listen, and along the way I'll tell you mine, but how we got here is not as important as how to get out of here.

Every addict has a story . . . or a bunch of stories, sometimes tailored to the audience. One story for the boss, another for the family, yet another for fellow alcoholics. Seems to me that the stories are all pretty much the same, they just shift the blame. To set the stage, let me tell my story crafted with you, the reader, in mind. You will, I guarantee, at times see yourself as if you were looking into a mirror. □

MY STORY

I was the middle child of nine in a first-generation Irish-American Catholic family, a family that reflected a recent-immigrant drive and the Catholic work ethic, determined to make it in this new world. My father was a lawyer and a politician—and president of the Board of Aldermen of a large mid-western city. When my mother stopped having babies she also became involved in politics, but as a campaign manager for a senator. Our family quickly went from pretty poor to quite well-off and living in a twenty-three room mansion.

But, as you will appreciate, achieving "success" took a lot of time and effort. Not much was left for the family, or, at least, for me. My parents rarely—maybe never—came to any of my games. They were not on hand when I won awards in school. They saw their role: to provide a clean home, plenty of food, tuition money, and strict rules of behavior.

Thus, I grew up neglected, needy. I was not

the classic "angry young man," I was the lost child. I didn't think that my parents even knew who I was; I wasn't good enough to merit their attention. Even though I was good in school— very good—I sensed that I would never measure up to my brothers and sisters. I stopped the pain—I didn't know any better—by being emotionally detached. I call it, "living alone in your head," where you are safe and no one can hurt you. You can make your own decisions and rationalize your actions. You punish yourself for your mistakes . . . or punish yourself for being just who you are.

Once, I did something at school—I don't even remember what it was, but it was not good—and I was caught by the nuns and sent home early. I didn't go straight home of course, but wandered around until the time I was supposed to arrive. It turned out that one of the nuns had called my mother to report the transgression, said they had sent me home early, and in the kind manner of nuns, everywhere, told her, "Tommy is a good boy, I'm sure it will all work out." When I got home, mother, of course, was waiting for an explanation and I, of course, denied that anything had happened. She said, "Listen, you have to learn how to tell the truth. If you're afraid of the consequences, always remember that telling the truth is the honorable thing to do."

So I admitted what I had done—and she gave me the spanking of my life. You can imagine the effect that had on my interest in truth-telling, certainly to my parents. In truth, as time went on I found myself laying down cover for anything I was going to do, even if it was something that would be totally OK with my parents. If I was going out with friend John, I would say, going to Mary's house to be with her brother. Misdirection, throw them off the scent. I don't actually know—actually, I doubt—if they ever tried to check up on me but the tactic made me feel safe. Safe was good, I was building a comfortable shell into which I could retreat, any time. And, as time went on, I discovered the complimentary value of pain-stopping (or pain-masking) substances.

I should have learned, early on, that I had what might be called an "addictive personality."

As a young child, I was a severe asthmatic. Whenever I took my medicine, I went hyper. My parents would rush me to the doctor. I rather liked being zonked . . .

I began smoking in the third grade. The gang at a local gas station got me started. I suppose they thought it was a great joke to see this little kid puffing away. I was quickly hooked and found a way to get my own supply. When I had money, I'd buy them at the drug store "for my father." When I didn't have money, I stole them. By the time I was in high school, I was doing at least a pack a day. Ten years later, I was up to two-and-a-half or three packs.

Booze? My parents were major-league entertainers. Almost every Friday and Saturday evening they would have people over for cocktails. My brother and I were the after-party clean-up detail, and I loved it. There was always something left in the glasses and I could take a sip here, a gulp there, not a lot, but enough to show me how much I liked it. When I was in the seventh grade, a buddy and I stole a bottle of Mogen David wine and drank it all. We got terribly drunk and sick. I didn't mind the sick part because I liked the drunk part.

By the time I was in high school, alcohol had become an important part of my life, aided and abetted by a friendly local bartender. He had once been in big trouble with the law and my uncle, a criminal defense attorney, had gotten his charges quashed. When the bartender discovered who I was, he seemed to think he could pay my uncle back by being nice to me. I could have sat in the bar drinking beer forever; I never had to pay. I have no idea why I was never busted as under-age, but this privilege endured for three or four years.

Well, I mis-spoke: I was busted, once. I went to an all-boys Catholic high school. Once a year they would have a "Day of Recollection," a one-day spiritual retreat with no regular classes. You were supposed to go to church or attend a few lectures. But no one was taking attendance, so I went to the bar. Well, one of the teaching Brothers was trolling the area, looking for truants, and there I was, ordering a beer. He pulled me out of the bar and led me back to school. And . . . that was it! A verbal slap across the knuckles with no follow-up. The school did not tell my parents.

Alcohol made me happy and brave and stupid. One time, at a basketball game, I thought it would be great fun to grab a trumpet from a member of the band and blow a congratulatory blast when one of our guys sank a basket. The principal came down from the stands and threw me out of the game; on Monday, summoned to his office, I learned that I was a disgrace to the school. Another time—I thought it would be great fun to stuff a freshman in a locker, except the hall was undergoing renovations. The locker wasn't anchored to anything and as he struggled to escape, the locker fell over and the freshman broke an arm. (Well, *he* didn't break it, I did.) I was suspended for a few days, probably should have been kicked out of school, but to my amazement—as with the Recollection Day event—the school did not tell my parents. Home free!

I should have been ashamed of myself— maybe I was, from those incidents and others— but I quickly learned how to suppress my guilt (if I was ever able to recognize it). Just chug down another pint or bottle or whatever and go to sleep. Wake up free, refreshed in mind body and spirit! The alcoholic's survival method of choice, at which I became a past-master.

Approaching graduation, I had won some pretty nice awards in speech and drama—but because of some other alcohol-fueled infraction I wasn't allowed to attend the ceremony and receive them. Since my parents were never actively involved in whatever I did at school and wouldn't have attended the ceremony anyway, they had no idea.

I was awarded a scholarship for a school of drama in California. Because of my father's obsession with the law, I was foreordained to be a lawyer whether I liked it or not. So I went to a local university and then on to law school. What had been occasional truancy in high school became the norm in college. I found that I didn't have to spend much time in class in order to get good grades, and it was much more interesting to share a few beers with some like-minded buddies at a near-by bar that catered to the college crowd.

In college and in law school—living at home and with my parents paying the tuition—I earned spending money from a variety of jobs. In the summer, daytime, I worked construction for a company owned by a political ally of my father. In the evenings and winter I parked cars in the nightclub area of town, where I made good money from tips. After getting off work at midnight, I spent it on booze, marijuana, and chasing girls.

I hear you asking: with all of that drinking, didn't you ever get into trouble?

Re-read above. My father was president of the Board of Aldermen. Sure, I would get hauled over by a cop, but my father was an icon with the police department—he was their pay-raise champion in the city government. The minute a cop would recognize my name, he would find a way to get me home, drive me, have his partner drive my car. The last thing they wanted was to upset my father by throwing his kid in jail. Yes, I got away with a lot of stuff.

I married Kate, the love of my life then and always, soon after I took the bar exam; then, I got a job and we settled into a routine . . . which for me included some heavy-duty late-night drinking. Over the years, living with my parents, my drinking had been regular but constrained. During our courtship, Kate knew that I drank, but in our social circle most of our friends also drank. With maybe a dozen years of practice, I was very good at keeping my drinking secret. Kate had no idea how much I drank or to what effect. Now I was free, so to speak, to expand on my practice. I drank enough during the day to keep sharp—at least, that's what I told myself. At night, after Kate had gone to sleep, my level of consumption rose, over time, to about half-a-fifth of vodka and a half-a-joint of marijuana.

I never got sloppy drunk or mean drunk or depressed drunk; quite the opposite. I was in a zone where I could work, read, function, be happy and stable, and do my job. But I was emotionally flat, literally anaesthetized from any true feelings. I lost my curiosity, avoided new experiences—the unsure and uncertain didn't challenge, they threatened. On the other hand, I was impulsive—I didn't think things through, I just bounced around. I followed no plan . . . daily or long-range . . . I looked forward to nothing except the next fix.

Only after I got into recovery, years later,

did I come to realize that the *real* reason—my *because*—I started drinking was to hide from reality. It was when I was sober that my nightmare would begin. My disease robbed me of the tools that I needed to live a happy, secure, carefree life.

Read on . . .

My first significant post-graduation employment was in Washington, D.C., in a world where drinking was a comfortable part of the job. I wanted to learn how the government worked, and became a staffer for a series of Senate committees, dealing every day with lobbyists who favored negotiating over the typical three-martini lunch. I was happy to be the negotiatee. A large part of my job was drafting legislation for the committee and writing speeches for the boss (the chairman). I believed that alcohol was the elixir that fueled my creative fire. The words just flowed.

Afternoons, my cronies and I might spend an hour or so contributing to the success of a local watering hole as we discussed the issues of the day. Many of the reporters who covered

Capitol Hill, with whom I had regular contact, carried pocket flasks and were always in a charitable mode. Had I given a thought to my own behavior, I would have rationalized . . . everyone was doing it, etc.

It was a great job, but after a couple of years or so, the boss—the committee chairman— announced that he was not going to stand for re-election, he was ready to retire; I didn't want to have to break in a new boss (truth be told, I didn't much like the logical successor), and I figured I'd probably learned enough about "how the government works." So I left Washington and went back home; I found a job with a big law firm, where the senior partner was the son of the U. S. Senator for whom my mother had been a campaign manager. A pressure job. I was motivated to prove my worth and I worked almost every Sunday, putting together briefs for the partners which were due on Monday. This was at a time when Sunday blue laws were in effect, the bars were closed and you couldn't buy booze. And I needed a drink. I always needed a drink, especially when I couldn't have one.

The law office was right in the middle of

downtown and across the street from a vacant lot that was the favorite gathering spot for homeless drunks and hoboes. God's truth, more than once I went down to join them, joking around, acting like I was one of the guys and oh, by the way, cadging a few swigs from someone's pint of whiskey. I guess I *was* one of the guys, just better dressed. Their generosity was real, we were all in the same boat and they knew it even if I didn't. One time I tried to hand a couple of bucks to my benefactor of the day. He didn't want to take it. The next time I joined them I provided the bottle.

One night, at a party, where the guests were skirting around the subject of using "drugs" when one of them said, "I have to tell you, you don't need to deal with shady suppliers of illegal substances, you probably already have some of the best drugs in your medicine cabinet." He was talking about a pain killer, Percodan, available from your friendly local pharmacist. As long as you had a prescription.

I didn't say anything ... but, yes, I had a bottle of Percodan in my medicine cabinet, left over from a back problem some time before. When I got home, already high from booze, I cut one pill in half to give it a test drive. It made me feel wonderful and I soon added Percodan to my nightly ritual that now became half a fifth of vodka, half a joint, topped off with half a pill that produced euphoria and then led me to sleep. When the pills ran out, you can bet that my "back pain" came back, big time, and my friendly local physician (who knew about my earlier problem) was innocently obliging. At the rate of half-a-pill, this supply lasted quite a while. □

TRANSITION

And then, lo and behold, my old boss at the senate changed his mind. He was not going to retire after all and asked if I would like to come back and rejoin his staff? Indeed. I was much more comfortable accepting free drinks from lobbyists than cadging drinks from homeless guys. I fell right back into my old routine. A lot of on-the-job imbibing, a bit of on-the-way-home socializing, followed by a nice dinner with my loving wife and, as time went on, our kids. Then, after dinner, I would retreat to my den, kill another half-fifth of vodka, knock off another speech, smoke a joint, then pop a diet pill for a quick fix and some blessed sleep for maybe five or six hours, then back up and at it again.

Diet pill? I had stopped pushing the "back pain" thing because someone told me that Percodan is addictive and hey, I didn't want to be addicted to anything. So I switched to diet pills, amphetamines. One of the older women on the staff (a motherly sort and a bit overweight) was my connection, always good for twenty or thirty pills. Half a pill was enough to take me back to the days of my youthful asthma, actually made me feel safe. A whole pill was even better. I'm lucky I didn't kill myself.

Did I ever have too much to drink, day or night? Of course, and it took some time for me to learn my limits, but along the way I don't believe I ever missed a day at work or an appointment because of booze. Hangovers? Yeah, until I learned to get everything in balance, but mine were more of a stomach than a head problem. Two or three beers at lunch were as good as Alka-Seltzer.

Did I not have some inkling that maybe I had a problem? Of course not. Oh, yes, I was a heavy drinker, but I was good at my job, I believed that alcohol contributed to my success and if things ever seemed to get a bit out of hand, they could easily be controlled. The proof? Came Lent—I always gave up alcohol. For forty days! Wow! Look at me! No problems, here. Of course, after Easter, right back at it.

But let me surprise you with proof that I could control alcohol. Permanently. With no outside help. After a total of six years with the Senate, I moved to a job as salesman at a major defense contractor back in my home town. Now, I freely admit that I didn't know much about selling, but since most of my work with the Senate had been in defense appropriations and I held the highest security clearances, I brought added value to the marketing department.

And the marketing department brought me world-wide travel and a whole new excuse for on-the-job socializing. At this, I was already a past master, but now I could do it at home *and* abroad. The job also put me in charge of a team of salesmen, and thus offered the healing power of arrogance—where, by making my subordinates feel small, I could feel big. I wanted people to *know* that I was in control, more powerful than any of them. I thought I was "motivating" the team but, of course, by putting them down I was really covering up my own insecurities. If I could have exercised any insight, I chose to remain blind.

Imagine the staff meeting, trying to salvage a failing program where someone, clearly, had to be at fault. I didn't care who, just "someone." As in, "You dumbshit, whoever told you that you should be a salesman?" Or, "You must be the dumbest person I've ever known," or, "That's the worst idea I've ever heard. Why would I ever want your opinion on anything?"

Once in a very rare time, someone would stand up to me, stand his ground, and I must submit—to my credit, I wasn't a total loser—I listened and assessed and often moved the renegade to a better job. As in one case, a guy who stood toe-to-toe and wouldn't back down, was promoted from a position as a minor staffer on one program to salesman-in-charge of another.

I wish I had more such examples, but, in truth, I had everyone living in fear of the next paycheck. And, in truth, in spite of such abysmal displays of "leadership," we made some improvements in the way the company did business and my team and I brought in a series of multi-million dollar contracts. I was on a roll . . . until . . .

I was offered a job with President Carter's 1980 re-election campaign . . . offered, by the president, in person, in the Oval Office, and I was stoked. I went back to my hotel to find a group of friends waiting in the bar—rumors spread fast in Washington—and the booze flowed as fast as the congratulations. At some point, I was headed out to the Men's Room when the desk clerk stopped me: "Mr. Gunn," he said, "You have an emergency call from your wife."

I called Kate, who had devastating news. Our eighteen-month-old daughter had been diagnosed with a serious disease. "How serious?"

"The doctor gives her eighteen months to live."

Through my drunken stupor, I went into shock, wandered out into the street. By accident—or some mysterious power—I found myself in front of the St. Matthews Cathedral. I stumbled over to the parish house and began banging on the door, sobbing, "Help me, help me." At last, a sleepy priest opened the door and I dug in my pocket, pulled out all of the money I had, maybe three hundred dollars and pleaded, "Father, you have to say mass for my daughter, she has an incurable disease, and I will pledge to God above never to drink another drop, never!"

A serious pledge to God is, well, a pledge. From that moment, I have never had a drop of alcohol . . . that was thirty years ago, and our daughter is alive, well, and thriving.

However . . .

Addiction is addiction. By 1985, I had survived five years without alcohol, I wasn't drinking and had stopped smoking pot. But I but hadn't given up the amphetamines, and to offset the booze I became hooked on Valium and was popping other pills as well. I don't even know what some of them were, things that friends would offer. As my addiction increased, so did my skill at hiding it . . . from my boss, my friends, and, most significant, from Kate and the kids. At least, I thought so.

Eventually, I had insight. I knew that the connection between my mind and my body had gone haywire, my normal coping strategies were ineffective and I was on the path to disaster. I met with a PhD psychologist someone told me about, identified as a world class expert on chemical dependency. I was expecting to get some sort of prescription, the non-professional's guess at a solution, pills to counter the pills. We talked for maybe fifteen minutes, not more than twenty, I told him my concerns, he asked me a few questions and then he looked at me said, "Tom, you are an alcoholic."

I said "What are you talking about? I haven't had a drop to drink in more than five years." He repeated, "You are an alcoholic" and I said "You're crazy." He said, well, I do see some issues, some things I think we can help you with. We have a very good program at the hospital, I'd like you to give it a try.

OK, I went along. I thought it was to give me some rest, take a few tests, wean me off the pills. At the hospital, they asked me to lie down on an examining table and gave me a shot that I later learned was to ensure that I didn't go into life-threatening withdrawal. When I woke up, I was outraged to discover that I was locked in the psychiatric unit at the hospital. Now, let me be clear, I was not Shanghaied, kidnapped and thrown into medical Hell. I had given "informed consent"—signed the papers—but with my habitual arrogance, I wasn't paying much attention. Until it was too late.

The chemical dependency program, they said, took twenty-eight days. After three days of sitting in a series of chemistry and "healthy nutrition" classes with a couple of over-aged hippies, I decided I'd had enough of that foolishness and decided to leave. I didn't do the logical thing, demand to be released, but I was not in a logical frame of mind. I would have to escape, as if I was the unjustly imprisoned hero in a movie. Of course, that was not going to be easy, there were bars on the windows—which eliminated the old tie-the-bed-sheets-together routine.

For non-staff visitors, entry into and out of the ward were controlled from the nurse's station; a non-staff visitor would ring a door buzzer, a video camera would take a look, and someone would trigger the switch that opened the door. Unless the buzzer sounded, no one ever looked at the video screen.

Staffers simply punched in a code on a key pad to enter or leave.

When we inmates—well, patients—were not in class or meeting with a doctor or social worker, we were supposed to be in our rooms, or we could sit in the little lobby near the entrance (which did triple duty as also the lunchroom and recreation center), watching television or reading magazines. I sat there long enough to catch the code—most of the staff were not careful; they were supposed to shield the key-entry process with their other hand, but most didn't bother. When the lobby was empty, I just walked up to the exit, punched in the code, and walked out. I took the stairs down to the ground floor of the hospital, to avoid running into someone on the elevator who might recognize me—but as I came out of the stairwell I spotted the head of the chemical dependency program standing at the end of the hall, by the front entrance. Whoops! Ever resourceful, I ducked into the nearest room.

And was confronted by maybe fifty people. A man standing at the front of the room—surely the meeting leader—said "Welcome, brother," and motioned me to an empty chair. Some other people turned around and repeated, "Welcome." A woman said "Good to see you," as if we were old friends. A bit confused, I sat down. I had nothing to lose in the room, loss of freedom waited out in the corridor.

Confusion turned to shock when another man stood up and said, "My name is John M and I am an alcoholic."

What had I gotten myself into? John proceeded to tell his story—he started drinking at 18 and was a full-blown alcoholic for more than twenty-three years, twenty of which he spent in the Army where he was a total screw up; had a series of DUIs, was busted in rank a couple of times, and was lucky to barely make it through to retirement. Next, free of whatever constraints military service had placed on him, he went through 6 jobs in 24 months. And oh, by the way, he had gone through two wives somewhere along the way.

"I tried AA once before," he said, and at least I now knew where I had landed: a meeting of Alcoholics Anonymous. "However," he continued, "it didn't work."

Finally, he said, he just was "sick and tired of being sick and tired" and went back to AA. "It's been a little more than a year—I know that's not very long, compared I'm sure with many of you—but it's been a wonderful year."

There were murmurs of affirmation, and in the spirit of the moment I guess I said "Good for you!" But to be honest, I couldn't much relate with John M. I'd never had any problems at work, never a driving violation, and, besides, I had already stopped drinking. I was just having momentary issues with other, well, "substances."

Next, the woman who had welcomed me stood up. "Hi, everyone. My name is Carrie

M and I am an alcoholic." She was a stay-at-home mother of three young children who had started out with an afternoon glass of wine while watching after-school television with the kids before her husband came home from work. Within a few years, without thinking—without really noticing—she had moved from one glass at four pm to starting at noon and going through—minimum—a bottle of wine, all before dinner time.

Over time, her husband began to notice something, but the changes were subtle, year to year or even month to month. She seemed to be mad at the world and began neglecting simple household chores, but she always had an explanation. She was "coming down with something," or just had an argument with her mother.

One afternoon, Carrie M. went out to the garage to recover a bottle she had hidden in a tool box, passed out, and fell to the floor. She was found, unresponsive, by her husband—who was frantic, having come home to find the kids watching TV but none of them knew where mommy had gone. He called 911; she was put in the 28-day program (which I had just, ah, left), followed by AA, and was now in her fifteenth year of sobriety.

She gave special thanks to her "higher power," whatever that was.

More murmurs of affirmation, and I joined in, but I still felt like an outside observer, not someone who was actually in the tent. Back when I was drinking, it had never been during the day except, well, for business meetings, and my pill-etc-popping was always after dinner during what I viewed as my "private time."

The last speaker introduced himself as "George N. I am an alcoholic physician, an anesthesiologist here at the hospital." His story was a bit different—he started on amphetamines in medical school, there was a ready supply, a lot of the students shared this seemingly minor vice. Pepped them up, kept them up to study, helped them meet the constant pressure. But he got hooked, and continued using after graduation by prescribing the pills for himself (well, he faked the scripts but ended up with the drugs). He had also discovered booze and became a major-league drinker as well, but had everything under control, no problem . . . until he made a mistake and a patient died.

Wow, talk about coming clean. He entered a treatment program for doctors (yes, he was not the only addicted medical professional), was granted a conditional license and earned his way back to full practice. By way of penance, he worked mostly pro-bono in a distressed neighborhood for four years. He acknowledged that he had been through serious family issues, especially with his kids, and while he was "ready" to be normal, it took some years of counseling for the rest of his family to trust him and join in. And now, he was "enormously happy." Thanks to AA.

There were the usual "affirming comments" but this time I didn't join it, my head was spinning; did I fit in here? I had been put into the rehab program—which I was trying to escape—because I was an addict—so they said—but I hadn't killed anyone, my family was just fine . . . weren't they?

These people were admitting to serious problems, addictions, but none of them claimed to be "cured," just to be "happy." Then suddenly, the meeting was over, everyone holding hands in a chain and reciting the "Our Father." This was followed by an enthusiastic joint holler of

"Keep Coming Back It Works If You Work It"

And then everyone shook hands with everyone in reach, many, reaching out to me. "Come back," some said. "We are here for you."

I had trouble processing all of this. I had just heard people admitting that they had totally screwed up their lives but had found a way out. People now displaying open honesty and humility about their problem. Two characteristics I don't think I had ever displayed, at least, not at the same time in the same conversation.

I may at times have been foolish, but I am not a fool. I finally "got it."

I realized that I really needed to—wanted to—stay in the treatment program, which presented an unusual problem: how to break back *into* the psych ward. I didn't have the courage to just go back and ring the buzzer. I took the stairs up and loitered in the hall outside the door—of course, I had already forgotten the key-code, so I had to wait to piggyback on someone going in. I tried to look busy, which was a neat trick because there was nothing to be busy with. But I managed, pretending to be deep in thought one moment, looking at my watch, starting for the elevator, whatever, and since no one else was in the hall for much more than a few seconds it worked. When a staffer came along to enter the ward—someone I had never seen, so I doubted that she would know who I was—I held the door open (she smiled and said, "Thanks"), slipped in right behind and went to my room. No one seems to have noticed that I was AWOL for almost two hours.

So, I not only went back—but paid attention. I learned a lot, of course, about the disease process and the typical impacts on health, life, and relationships. And I gained helpful insight into an issue that had been following me around most of my life—as I noted earlier, a feeling of total inferiority, of being a worthless human being. Well, I guess I was not alone: a therapist gave my problem a name, "toxic shame."

This is not to be confused with feelings of guilt, which more properly are involved with some transgression, some socially-unacceptable act (as when I put the freshman into the locker or blew the trumpet at the game). Shame grows out of the certain knowledge that you are unworthy, a generally bad person. As one counselor told me, "Guilty people fear they will be punished. Shamed people fear they will be abandoned."

Toxic shame can take many forms, including a sort of paralysis (an inability to do anything), or a need to escape your normal environment and seek out places where you can be alone and unseen, or a compulsion to put on a smiling face as a mask to cover your terror, or an obsession with perfection—if you always do everything *right,* never make a mistake, your secret will be safe.

In my case, it may have been manifest in my need to always be "in charge," superior, always the critic, never the target of criticism. And most certainly was one of the underlying reasons I began drinking so much, so early in life.

I didn't make it out in twenty-eight days. I was not the perfect student, and needed more time, three more days, as I recall, which caused no end of trouble with the insurance company. There were twenty-two people with me in the hospital program. Sad to say, without additional and on-going treatment of one sort or another, many if not most of them were not able to stay sober. About one-third of the group went right back to drinking the minute they were released;

I think all of them are dead. Another one-third made it for maybe a year before relapse and some never recovered. Of the final onethird—a group that included me—most have remained sober and most have been active in AA.

I attended the hospital AA meeting for more than three years and got to know, respect and love each of these fellow addicts. They loved me when I was feeling so guilty and incompetent and just could not find a way to love myself. I found some other meetings I liked as well and attended all, sometimes as many as four a week. I found that I really needed the extra support.

I had taken the first steps on the road to recovery . . . but it was to become a very steep, very long, difficult, but exhilarating journey. I wish I could report that suddenly, everything was wonderful and I marched forward, head held high, ready to take on my disease—hey, the world!—and win. To the contrary, for a while I was so devastated by the realization of just how much I had let my friends and family down that I hit an emotional bottom and wanted to get away—permanently. I even bought a gun, put it in the trunk of my car, ready. Just in case.

One day, I was so angry with God that I

drove to the cathedral. "You have to understand something," I said to God, "this is all bullshit, I need a sign that I'm going to be OK, that I will be able to make it up to my wife and kids and get on with life. I need a sign, I'm talking, like the statue of the Blessed Mother turning and looking at me."

Well, nothing happened. Still angry, I went back to my car. There was a pack of cigarettes on the seat, and I knew I needed a smoke while I figured out the next step. I grabbed a cigarette, pushed in the lighter and . . . I swear, a voice came out of the blue, "You don't need that." And without thinking, I answered, "Listen goddamn it I'm not taking about smoking I'm talking about being happy." And it clicked—this was the sign! I quit. Forever. I'd been smoking two and a half to three packs a day for my whole adult life and I threw the cigarettes out of the window and have not had a desire to smoke since that day.

One step at a time . . .   □

EVERYBODY DRINKS

Not quite. So let's start with some basics. More than one-third of adult Americans never drink. About the same number drink, but at "low risk" levels, defined by the National Institutes of Health (NIH) as—for men, no more than four "standard" drinks on any given day but no more than fourteen drinks in a week; for women, three in a day, no more than seven in a week. (Older men—over the age of 65—are advised to follow the women's rule.)

"Women's rule" — only *half* the weekly ration for men? Let me here raise a gender-specific warning flag: women metabolize alcohol at a different rate than men, get drunker faster, and develop cirrhosis of the liver at a higher rate than men. . . in fact, according to the National Institute on Alcohol Abuse and Alcoholism, alcoholic women have significantly higher death rates—from accident, disease, or suicide—than their male peers. (*Female reader:* do I have your attention, now?)

Non-drinkers and low-risk drinkers add up

to seven in ten adults. This leaves a lot of us who at one time or another put health, wealth, and the general welfare at risk. May I assume that you join me in this group?

This does not automatically make you an alcoholic. I know a lot of folks who drink a lot more than the guidelines, and they well may be damaging their health, but they can pretty much take the booze or leave it alone. A second DUI may scare them into near-sobriety, or a "final warning" from the boss, or, really scary, if they wake up in bed with a stranger . . . and not for the first time.

Here's what should be another sobering thought: alcohol is not a solitary (and yes, sometimes social) recreation, affecting only the drinker. Not to be preachy, but the universe of people negatively impacted may be four or five times the number of problem drinkers. Family members, co-workers and employers, innocent victims of an automobile accident. Victims of crime—according to some reports, almost 75 percent of felonies are alcohol-related. Then, there are the non-violent but potentially devastating effects such as accidental pregnancy.

I'm sure you can figure it out.

But perhaps the most sobering of all: being put on notice by a physician who says, "Just looked over your brain-scan MRI and have to tell you, I see some problems. How much alcohol do you drink?"

So . . . where do we go from here?

Let's set the stage. "Standard" is an important concept, because most of us don't pay much attention. Across beverages, there is about same amount of alcohol in 1.5 ounces of whiskey, 5 ounces of wine, and 12 ounces of beer. When, may I ask, was the last time you measured hard liquor with a shot glass? Bet you just dump the booze over the ice or mostly fill an oversized goblet with wine. (By the way, they make those large goblets, up to 22 ounce or thereabout, to allow 5 ounces of wine to develop layers of aroma, the "bouquet." Do you ever bother to savor the bouquet? Do you even know what it is?) And, how often do you top-off a drink before the glass is empty? Honest answer?

Beer may be the only beverage that is easily measured, twelve ounces at a time. At least, you can count the empty cans in the morning.

However, just as not everyone who drinks a lot is an alcoholic, not every alcoholic drinks too much. It's not the quantity, it's the quality. More than a hundred years ago, someone coined the term "dipsomaniac" (from the Greek, roughly: "thirsty and crazy"). *Dipsomania* is an irresistible urge to drink anything but usually alcohol and was a thread of Victorian tales of horror, a Jekyll and Hyde moment. You know the story: the respectable Dr. Jekyll discovered a potion that, when ingested, turned him into the evil Mr. Hyde. What you probably don't know is that author Robert Louis Stevenson was, well, a dipsomaniac and the story is an allegory for the curse of alcoholism and English attempts to control it. The name, "Jekyll"? No fiction, here: Lord Jekyll was the man who helped lead the Temperance Movement.

The dipsomaniac's beverage of last resort is probably Ethylene Glycol—which you may know as the main constituent of anti-freeze but is a compound found in some other products, including paint and cosmetics. In its pure form it is colorless, odorless, sweet-tasting. It does produce blessed intoxication, followed a few hours later by some combination of nausea, vomiting, convulsions, stupor, or coma. As little as four ounces may be enough to kill an average sized man. Call it, the last resort of dipsomaniacal desperation.

Let us hope that most users and abusers are not clinically stupid (although that assumption is, well, problematic), but one operative definition of an alcoholic is a person who *must* have a drink, cannot be comfortable until having that drink, even if only one martini a month.

Self Help

If you are a problem drinker, measurement—keeping track—is a good start for any stop-or-reduce drinking effort. If you know how much you are actually drinking and it is above the guidelines, you—rational you—can conform. Make a simple checklist, at 6:00 pm, just home from work, loving spouse greets you with a martini. ("Thanks! I needed that!") 6:45, another martini. Dinner: Glass of wine . . . or two. After dinner, a bit of TV, hey, another glass of wine. And? Oh, yeah, forgot about the beer — well, two beers—at lunch

If this works and you can moderate intake, say, cut out at least one beer at lunch, the second martini, and all after the first "glass of wine," you may be headed toward the winner's circle. In fact, this may be a pretty good test, a bit of self-induced diagnosis. Are you or are you not, an alcoholic? If you *are,* this keeping track might last for about a day and a half. Then you will know it's time for a different approach.

You are not alone. More than 700,000 Americans get alcohol-related treatment on any given day in one form or another (sometimes in combination or sometimes alone and there is little clinical agreement as to what may or may not be "most effective"). The point is, some things may work for one person, some for others. We'll run through all of them.

Where to start?

Before you expose yourself to strangers (trust me: your friends and family already know) you might want to run a private evaluation. I can give you one, right here, called **"CAGE"** (from the first letter of each key item), suggested by the Hazelden Foundation:

☐ Have you ever felt you should **CUT DOWN** on your drinking?

☐ Have people **ANNOYED** you by criticizing your drinking?

☐ Have you ever felt **GUILTY** about your drinking?

☐ Have you ever had a drink first thing in the morning as an **EYE OPENER** to steady your nerves or get rid of a hangover?

Answer yes to two of the four, you may need help. As if you didn't already know. If that seems too simplistic, here are a few more questions to ponder:

☐ Have you ever tried to stop using alcohol or drugs?

☐ Has anyone close to you expressed concern about your alcohol or drug use?

☐ Do you find it difficult to have a good time without using alcohol or drugs?

☐ Do you spend a lot of time thinking about ways to get alcohol or drugs?

☐ Have you ever experienced a loss of memory because of drinking?

☐ Have you ever made a promise to yourself that you will quit or cut down on your drinking and then found yourself not keeping the promise you made?

Counseling

Your personal journey to recovery may start with your friendly local primary health care professional. You likely will get a little lecture on the "standard" drinks and recommended levels of consumption (which, I dare say, as a concerned drinker or a fast reader—see above—you already know). Health care professionals have little guides, some even in pocket size so they will always be armed and ready even in a social situation. "Recommend lower limits or abstinence," they are advised. "Express openness to talking about alcohol abuse." There follow eleven probing questions such as: do you have trouble at work, trouble at home, trouble with the law, clear health impairment, can't stop drinking no matter what? If you answer "Yes" to maybe a third of them, you will be told that you are a candidate for more intense counseling. As if you didn't already know.

So, if you really want to take a positive step forward, you might skip the family practice and move right on to consultation with a substance abuse specialist, someone to sort out and try to make sense of your specific situation. Which of the more common risk factors, or socially unacceptable activities, apply to you?

☐ Alcoholism runs in the family. Current generation only, or further back?

☐ Started drinking at an early age? Heavy smoker?

☐ Smoke other substances, most illegal?

□ Any other addictions? Cocaine, opiates, pain-killers?

□ Suffer from other psychiatric illness—depression, chronic anxiety, bi-polar disorder?

□ Any specific problems that may be attributed to drinking? (The most embarrassing and probably the hardest to answer.)

□ Have you tried to stop or cut back on your own?

□ Have you ever sought outside help? If so, in what form?

Pharmacotherapy

You would think, there must be a pill, somewhere, that will block the urge to drink. There are a few medications that have proven helpful for some people, at some time. In clinical trials, one drug reduced the consumption for early-onset alcoholics (those who started drinking heavily before age 25) but did not affect later-onset alcoholics; another drug seems to work the other way around. One drug may reduce craving, another encourages the avoidance of alcohol by triggering nausea from as small a quantity of alcohol as might be found in salad dressing or mouthwash. All medications come with grave cautions and predictable side-effects. This is something for discussion between you and a professional.

Psychotherapy

Having assessed your situation, the counselor may suggest one-on-one therapy. I strongly recommend that addicts see an expert in chemical dependency for as long as a year, two years, if they can afford it (and a lot of insurance companies will pay for it). You will walk through your life, point by point, to find out why you did certain things and discuss the current daily challenges that lead you to drink. You will be taught skills to cope with problems and strategies to change harmful patterns of behavior. Not just "count the drinks" but how to ask for help from family and friends (avoid offering you a drink, stop the carping, and give you a chance to work it out). You will be encouraged to develop social relationships where drinking is not a major component.

Your therapist may recommend a temporary stay in a residential unit with a more intense dose of education—or put you on some medication, or have you hook up with a mutual-help group. The best-known is Alcoholics Anonymous. On my personal story, as you may recall, I visited a therapist to seek advice about drug abuse, and he put me in an in-hospital treatment program—a big surprise, and not what I expected but it led to my discovery and acceptance of Alcoholics Anonymous.

For the record: other mutual-help groups include Moderation Management, Secular Organizations for Sobriety, SMART Recovery, and Women for Sobriety. Alcoholics Anonymous saved my life. I have no experience with or opinion about any of the others.　□

ALCOHOLICS ANONYMOUS

Launched in the 1930s, AA grew out of the experience of two men who met almost by chance, discovered they had a mutual problem with alcohol, and admitted to each other that they couldn't control their drinking on their own and discovered the value of mutual support and understanding. Soon, more alcoholics were brought into that tent until today, there are almost two million members loosely organized in more than 100,000 groups, world-wide.

"Loosely" is an operative phrase. AA has no formal organization; call it a federation without leaders. No elected or appointed officers. No big budget. There is a headquarters of sorts with some seventy-five paid staffers who handle requests for information and maintain a web site, but who have no authority over the members. Members of each group take turns leading the meetings, handling any administrative issues (like, making sure the rent is paid—money for which largely comes from passing the hat at meetings).

There are some general "rules" of behavior and operation—notably, take no position on public or political controversies of the day. The baseline philosophy is presented in a book, *Alcoholics Anonymous*, known as the "Big Book" (because the original edition was printed on heavy paper stock, making for a thick volume). Members are not required to read the Big Book, although it does offer useful encouragement and suggestions to aid in recovery.

The only requirement for joining AA is a desire to stop drinking.

Over the years, AA developed—and refined—an outline to guide the recovery efforts of alcoholics. Members should attend regular meetings; having another, experienced member as a "sponsor" can be of value; members should (but are not required to) work through a step-by-step self-discovery process, which suggests a focus on one issue at a time. AA calls theirs "The Twelve Steps" (and with very minor modifications, it is also used in the similar mutual-help groups Narcotics Anonymous, Al-Anon, Alateen, Gamblers Anonymous, Nicotine Anonymous, Dual-Recovery Anonymous, and

Adult Children of Alcoholics).

AA created a matching template, the "Twelve Traditions," which reiterates core issues of the Twelve Steps in the broader concept of AA as a whole.

The Meeting

The meeting is home base for AA. You should have a home group, in a place and time certain, that you attend much of the time—size doesn't matter, it may have a dozen or three hundred members. Once you start attending meetings, once you commit yourself to healing, it won't take long for you to feel the comfort, the closeness, the protection of the group. The meeting is a place where you can be at ease and start to shed the terrible aspects of your disease—and learn to live. AA is a fellowship, where the members share much more than social camaraderie. We are bonded by the tragedies in our past and the purpose of the present.

I grew up in a culture where people were judged—by whatever measure, other than race. We were truly color blind, but social snobs. Status seemed important, having money was a plus. If someone wasn't successful, we didn't have much time for them. In my Senate job, I became keenly aware of titles, status, because we played to power. Elected officials were easily identified (and anyone called "chairman" moved to the head of the line). I soon enough learned to decipher the corporate pecking order ("vice president of" is senior to "director of" which is senior to "manager of" who lords it over "supervisor of") and spot subtle signs of standing: did the executive arrive in a chauffeur-driven company car, or in a taxi? Who held the door open for whom? I suppose in the real world this may make sense because someone is always in charge, someone is empowered to make the decisions, and you need to know who that someone might be.

However, for an alcoholic, a focus on status —especially your own—becomes a serious distortion—a distraction—that gets in the way of recovery. Many people come into the program wearing their status on their sleeve, sometimes literally, in a high-class bespoke suit. Wearing wrist watches bought from a jeweler rather than Wal-Mart, driving an upscale car, everything screaming, "Look at me! I'm successful!"

I know this full well. Once I was out of the sheltering world of my parents, I was driven to prove to them, to anyone, that I could make it on my own. My self-esteem was tied to what other people thought of me (or what I *thought* they thought of me, as triggered by the status symbols I scattered liberally along the path), not what I thought of myself.

"Look at me! I'm successful!" Yeah, maybe, but not very successful at dealing with the single most important factor of my life: I was an addict and all addicts are equal in the eyes of the Lord. And of each other. And the "meeting" is the proving ground.

You're not limited to attending one specific meeting, you could sample dozens. I have attended four different meetings in a week just in my hometown. Each offers a different set of friends and supporters.

Any given meeting may be organized to best suit the needs of various populations served (clearly identified in print or on-line listings).

Some meetings are broad but basic: "Open" to anyone interested in observing or sampling AA in action, or "Closed" to anyone except alcoholics who have a desire to stop drinking. There may be subsets: men only, women only, couples only, young people, health care professionals, gay or lesbian (which may be identified by the code words "Live and Let Live"). Special features may be listed, such as "interpreter for the hearing impaired," or a meeting in Spanish, or wheelchair accessible, or child care available. Or any combination, one or all.

Any given meeting may have a special focus: Beginners, running through the basics; Big Book meeting, where the group studies one or another of the AA guiding principles; Open Discussion, to take on specific issues; Step Discussion, to work through one step (or even a portion of a step); similar, a discussion of the AA Traditions; or a combination "Steps & Traditions" discussion; a Speaker meeting, to listen to and question an individual authority or experienced member of AA. But a caution: any AA meeting is restricted to the discussion of alcoholism and attendant problems. This is not the place to seek guidance or support for other addictions; there are specific programs that focus on those.

In a large metropolitan area, you can probably find one or more meetings in any of the categories, broad or narrow, on any given day. Smaller cities and towns will likely concentrate on the typical population served but even then there may be once-a-month gatherings of a special community.

To Find a Meeting

In days gone by, you might consult the AA directory, "Where and When," which catalogued meetings—location, day or date and time, type of meeting (open, closed, whatever), and program notes. If traveling, Yellow Pages were key: you would look for a near-by church (denomination of your choice, although I found that Catholic and Episcopal churches would be most likely to have a meeting at least once a week) and make a phone call or two. Any church office should have information on meetings scheduled at other churches.

But today, you just hop on the internet and

do a quick search. You will be rewarded with location (with map) of every meeting in the area you designate along with schedules, criteria, features, program, smoking or non (here "non" has become the norm), and special instructions ("Use door through east gate; M-F meet in Heartland Hall; Saturday in room 26"). That's quite useful for anxious beginners when confronted by very large churches or community centers. Which, indeed, is the right door and where is the right room? Your typically anxious beginner will not be likely to ask directions from strangers in the parking lot.

This internet guidance works in many if not most modern nations where the internet is king. However . . . what about those countries that are more or less open to the internet but where the consumption of alcohol is banned (or, at the least, is barely tolerated for non-citizens)? Some Muslim countries (Singapore, Kuwait) allow a few Christian churches where meetings might be held; in others (Saudi Arabia), where Westerners are housed in reasonably self-contained compounds, you might have dinner meetings in someone's home.

But here, the internet comes into play as more than just a locating tool. If it is not practical to have physical meetings, you can have a virtual, on-line version. While traveling, over many years and at one time or another, I have attended on-line meetings with folks who were stationed in Saudi Arabia, Kuwait, Dubai, Abu Dhabi, and Singapore, all at the same time. We had a "chat room" (this was long before any of the social networking initiatives), not at any fixed address but changed from one session to the next. The coordinator would send out an email announcement, and I could sit in my hotel room and participate.

For me it was a convenience, I was never in any troublesome country all that long, but for some of the participants, who were stationed in those countries for a year or more, this was a lifeline.

On The Ground

Wherever you attend a meeting you will be welcomed and made to feel at home: there is a suggested order, a schedule to be followed. Time honored and time-tested. Everything in its place. One step at a time. The chair of the meeting (who may be assigned for just this meeting, or may be doing this for a month) will open with the serenity prayer:

God grant me the serenity to accept the things I cannot change; courage to change the things I can; and wisdom to know the difference.

The members will be asked to identify themselves, "I'm John B. and I'm an alcoholic." The admission—"I am an alcoholic"—is a key part of recovery, entered into right up front with Step One (see below). "First name (and maybe last-name initial) only" is a ritualistic pass at maintaining the anonymity of the members. As a practical matter, you may not be anonymous at all, there may be people in the meeting who know you, but they will not be likely to spread your secret outside of the meeting where "trust" is one of the most important components of AA and your privacy is sacrosanct. "Not be likely" is of course a qualifier; mistakes happen. One happened to me [page 96] but since I entered recovery, I have never tried to hide my disease. Quite the contrary: I want to do anything I can to spread the word; you are reading one part of that effort.

The body of the meeting may follow a number of program formats, as noted above, such as a discussion, a study of the Big Book, a review of one of the Twelve Steps, whatever. Members who have reached an anniversary point—one year or a dozen—will be acknowledged and usually given a token, a special birthday coin. At some point, at one meeting or another and, over time, at many more meetings, you will be encouraged to tell your story.

Comes the Hard Part

Now that you know more about AA, you've found a meeting that seems right for you, and you've made the big decision: you are going to the meeting and you're going to come clean.

But . . . ah, how clean? You are committed to telling the truth, so far as it goes. Your dilemma: do you make it seem really bad so people will feel sorry for you, or do you fudge things a bit so they will think you are not as sick as you really are? Indeed, the hardest part of recovery may be telling the truth, because you long ago forgot how. For an addict, lying means survival. Even simple questions bring pause, like from your boss, "Do you have the report ready?" The report that was due yesterday before, oh, your car broke down or—yes!—the company email system must be screwed up. From your son, "Why did you miss my game yesterday? Oh, just repeat the broken-car excuse.

Or, perhaps, sometime, you've had an auto accident—for real—and your insurance company, inquires, "Can you tell us the details?" Some drunk came out of nowhere, hit me, and kept going. From your spouse, "Did you see the grocery money? I swear I put it on the table last night." Maybe one of the kid's friends pinched it off (little pun, there, because you traded the grocery money for a bottle of that Scotch whisky called "Pinch") If you tell the truth, you lose. You reach a point where you will go to great lengths to keep anyone from knowing what you are thinking or doing, no matter how benign.

What, indeed, is "truth"? Pick your favorite definition: "accuracy, actuality, authenticity, candor, conformity to fact, correctness, exactness, fact, honesty, integrity, precision, probity, realism, reality, right, sincerity." To which we could add a corollary word, "trust." Things that make up the social contract, without which we would all revert to barbarianism and the lack of which have been destroying your life.

Sponsors

Working with and through AA is not something you must do alone. You will have the support of everyone in the group, each of whom as been through the same process. And you will have the one-on-one direct support of a "sponsor"— someone to literally hold your hand and guide your steps as you walk through the difficult process of recovery. Your sponsor will not be your new best friend or a substitute for a drinking buddy. Your sponsor is to be your mentor, your champion, your guide through the Twelve Steps—the person who will lift you up when you have fallen and give you a kick in the pants when you have strayed. Your sponsor is not a professional therapist, substitute priest, marriage counselor, or social worker. Your sponsor, in so many words, is just another addict in recovery, but someone who has already been down the path, who may have stumbled a few times along the way, and knows how to avoid the potholes.

You don't need to have a sponsor, it is not a condition of membership in AA, but I think anyone would be foolish not to take advantage of the experience, wisdom, and compassion they have to offer. The meeting supports your struggle, your sponsor helps you understand how to change your life, walks you through the Steps and gives you a plan to deal with your pain.

How to find a sponsor? Often, they will find you, the newbie standing out on the crowd as someone who could use a little support. Or the meeting leader, as part of the agenda, will often announce, "Anyone need a sponsor, raise hands. Anyone willing to sponsor?" The initial match-up should in my judgment always be regarded as temporary, to avoid hurt feelings later if the marriage doesn't work out. And if it does, great, it's as permanent as either party wants it to be.

Thus, you would typically get a sponsor out

of your home group—someone who hears your stories and comes to know you well enough to tune in to your evasions. Initially, your sponsor may set a rigorous task to ensure your commitment and prove your interest: often, for someone new to the program, it might be a mandate to do "ninety meetings in ninety days." That could be one a day, or three on one day and none for the next few days, whatever works, but this forces a focus—which is one key tactic in combating the disease.

Your sponsor likely will propose a schedule for face-to-face meetings—every Monday at lunch or every Wednesday evening, say, over coffee. Over at least the first few weeks—or months—your sponsor may ask you to call every day to talk about whatever is on your mind. For example, on my daily report I might say to my sponsor, "I really beat up on this guy today" (figuratively, of course, by dumping on him in a staff meeting. You know, "You idiot! What ever made you think you could do this job?"). My sponsor would ask, "Why?" Why, indeed? I'd never had to confront the "why." Why was I so often sarcastic, demeaning, overpowering? Well

. . . probably because I was insecure, I wanted everyone to know that I had my act together, and I wanted to be sure that they all—targets and witnesses alike—KNEW how powerful I was. The more snide and hurtful the putdown, the better I felt. About myself. Toxic shame, to the rescue.

It took a long time. But I learned . . .   □

THE TWELVE STEPS

The Twelve Step Program helps you sort out the things for which you are responsible from those over which you have no control, to keep a focus on changing what you can, one day at a time, one step at a time, usually (but it's not mandatory) in numerical order. Usually, you would be guided through the steps by your sponsor. It is, in my judgment, the true key to success in AA. Meetings are good, fellowship is important, but the Steps take you to victory. And keep you there. People who drop out of AA, who fall back—and there are many—just don't get it.

Pay attention. If you take anything away from my book, it is this: you must fully participate in the program. *All* of the Steps. Not just this year or next, but forever. It is worth it.

Step One - *We admitted we were powerless over alcohol--that our lives had become unmanageable.*

I was brought up to believe that if you try hard enough, fight hard enough, you will always win—the American dream. But under AA, you have to surrender right up front, and accept that you are powerless. You can fight all you want, but you will only be fighting yourself. And there will be no winner. One of my sponsors put it this way: "Tom," he said, "You used to box" Yes, he knew me well, I had been a "Golden Gloves" competitor. "Can you imagine." my sponsor asked, "waking up every day, suiting up and getting in the ring with Muhammad Ali? And getting the stuffing knocked out of you? Every day? How long would it take for you to realize that you need to find something else to do with your life."

Addicts live in denial, there's nothing wrong that another drink or pill won't fix. At some point, many, if not most, will admit—even if only to themselves—that they have a problem (and I'm willing to bet that you have done so once, or many times). You can try a workaround—sure, a lot of people do— bring in the counselor, crank up the willpower, and find the "proper balance" where every now and then a drink, pill, whatever is just fine.

In my experience, that level of "fine" is never reached. And *you* know it. If willpower had worked for you, you wouldn't still be reading my book. I don't discount the value of counseling (my recovery began with the 28-day treatment), and I firmly believe that professional counseling should be part of any recovery program. Work with an expert in chemical dependency for a year, two if you can afford it (often covered by insurance). Go through your life point by point, discover why you did certain things, discuss daily challenges, learn the triggers that lead you to drink, all very helpful.

But counseling as the cure? Let me say it again: if you tried it and it worked, you wouldn't be reading this book. So let's deal with our mutual reality. The breakthrough comes when "we," you and me, admit that our addiction is so out of control that, try though we might, we are powerless to change. It's absolutely crazy: by using, we throw away those things that should be most important to us in our lives—our relationships with family and friends, our honesty, and any respect that we may have earned somewhere along the way.

Thus, Step One. We accept the fact of our disease. And acknowledge, to ourselves, to the group, that we need help. We may have started using for different reasons, our individual "because," but have all ended up at the same place, unable to measure and moderate. We finally realize that we indeed have a disease that cannot be cured by rational behavior—except the hyper-rational move of hooking up with AA.

Step Two - *Came to believe that a Power greater than ourselves could restore us to sanity.*

Step Three - *Made a decision to turn our will and our lives over to the care of God as we understood Him.*

Step One helps you get sober, Steps Two and Three begin the process of living sober. You now understand that your life is fully screwed up and that you have been unable to do anything about it—except make it worse. You know that you need help, and you're not afraid to ask for it.

Perhaps the least understood and most controversial aspect of AA is the idea that alcoholics should surrender to a "higher power." Uh-oh, is this some sort of cult? Many people I have sponsored got through Step One with ease but grew restive at Step Two, turned off by any idea that AA was "religious." Be assured: while the word "God" is frequently used, it is often modified with a clarifying "as we understand Him." There are atheists, agnostics, and Buddhists in AA, members without distinction. For some, the higher power is the group.

The best advice I ever got came from my first sponsor. He said, "I have never been a religious person but I know how important it is to stay connected to my higher power. Every day, I say two special prayers: in the morning, in the shower, I say, out loud: 'God, let me stay sober for one more day and let me treat everyone I meet today, the way I would like to be treated.' Then every night just before going to bed, I say, "God, thank you for letting me stay sober for the day, forgive me—help me to forgive myself—for anything I have done that was not up to our standards, and if I die in my sleep, please take me home."

I had drifted away from my church—when I did go to mass, I spent more time grading the "performance" and critiquing the sound system than in listening to the message. My prayer life was more or less limited to asking God to keep me from having a drink . . . when I was about to walk into a bar. Didn't work, of course, so I was a bit skeptical about Step Three. But I accepted my sponsor's advice on faith, and vowed to emulate his routine. I have done so every single day since. The prayer in the morning puts a focus on my disease and my commitment; at night, it also allows me to cast off my guilt should I have done something to hurt, demean, or offend anyone.

We live in a world where we are always being judged for good or ill; parents are judgmental; employers are judgmental; angry spouses can be judgmental. Let me submit: the most important influence in your life should be a non-judgmental God or special "higher power," however you define it. My personal theology has evolved and is very simple: God loves me, just the way I am and forgives me for what I have done. Knowing that gives me the strength to make amends and grow, not in God's eyes, but in my own.

Pay attention: there is only one person who will be with you, for good or ill, throughout your entire life. That is *you*, and you would be much better off if you learn to love yourself. Next, how about, love others as you would have them love you? Sound familiar? Nothing new, here, it's a concept that animates many if not most religions of the world.

And it is at the heart of AA.

About six months into the program, I was really feeling bad and it showed. After one meeting, one of the Old-Timers came over and asked if I might do him a favor. "Tomorrow morning," he said, "I have to go somewhere do you think you could give me a ride? Meet me here at the club, 10 o'clock? It won't take long."

I said, "Sure." So I picked him up and he directed me to a small business district. Across the street was a little Catholic chapel. He said, "I won't be long. Why don't you go on in there, it's run by the Carmelite nuns, I think you'll really like it."

He was right. It was very serene, and I stood in front of the altar and said a prayer, something rote out of my childhood but it took me back to when I was more active in the faith and I felt, literally, as if I was being wrapped in the spirit. When I came out, Old Timer was waiting in the car and after I drove us back to the club, he pulled a small book out of his pocket and handed it to me: title, "Came to Believe." It was a narrative of the spiritual adventures of a bunch of AA members. I was grateful, and found the book of great value: it did indeed help me focus on some of my issues. I assumed it was a thank-you for the transportation.

About a month later, I was on my way home from work and decided to drop in on a meeting that I knew was going on at the club. When I walked in, the Old Timer was speaking, talking about how important the program had been in his life even though he was an atheist. I was dumfounded. After the meeting, I went up and asked, "You are an atheist?" and he said, "Yes, my higher power is the program."

"You brought me to the chapel and you gave me that book. . ."

"Tom," he said, *"you're* not an atheist. In our program, you have to give people the tools *they* need."

I cried all the way home.

Step Four - *Made a searching and fearless moral inventory of ourselves.*

Step Five - *Admitted to God, to ourselves, and to another human being the exact nature of our wrongs.*

After finishing Step Three, I felt liberated, I had help and support, and I thought the hard part was over. Not quite . .

At one of our weekly sessions, my sponsor asked, "Well, what have you been doing today?" Without thinking, I gave him my usual report—with a stupid touch of pride—how I really beat up on one of my team, let him have it, let him know how worthless he was, what a waste of money.

My sponsor gave me a strange look, and not for the first time, asked, "Why?"

"Because . . ." My sponsor and I had already been through this, in earlier discussion, that the "because" had nothing to do with my victim, but that I was having a bad day, perhaps one of our contract proposals had been challenged, and I was feeling very insecure, so I yelled at this guy to let him know that I was in charge!

As my sponsor already knews, I had been doing this sort of thing for years. But now I was really involved in the program, going through the Steps, and my sponsor said, "OK, time for Step Four."

Step Four: you must take a personal inventory, going back as far as you can remember. Write down everything bad you have ever done, every mean comment you have ever offered, list every person you have ever hurt. Well, other than the guy I just beat up on, I didn't think I would have much to record and suggested, perhaps, that I could skip this step. My sponsor said, "No."

OK, so I went to a bookstore that specialized in addiction paraphernalia and bought a workbook, complete with blank forms to be filled in, key words to trigger thought. I set aside some private time, sat down, and began writing. I wrote about lying to my wife, my parents and friends. About ignoring my children. About making excuses rather than admitting guilt. How I shared unsupported gossip at the workplace to hurt co-workers. How I lied on my expense reports to cover up drinking bouts. Before I knew it, I had filled three workbooks and it took me six weeks to get all of my thoughts assembled in a fashion that I hoped would meet my sponsor's approval when I sat down for Step Five. He had become a surrogate parent, firm but caring, and I was the child eager to please.

We go through life so much into ourselves, so self-focused, that we forget—if we ever really knew—the effect we have on other people and the importance of relationships. Step Four is designed to bring us down to earth and boy, does it ever! I was forced to remember all of the wrongs I had committed, how much I had hurt my loved ones, my friends, and co-workers.

And myself. It knocked me for a loop. In truth, I almost gave up. There were things, many things, that I just did not want to dredge forth; how many times I had lied to the people I loved, how many times I had been cruel to people who did nothing to deserve my disdain or wrath. Things that I had buried away, on purpose . . . that I now was expected to resurrect?

I asked my sponsor, again, why not just stay at Step Three and focus on my higher power? All I wanted to do—was ready to do, had admitted I needed to do—was to stop using. He said "Give me your report."

And so I did, when ready, in a four-hour-long presentation. I finished, exhausted but strangely euphoric. I now understood: I was leaving behind a life of smoke and mirrors, of shuffling facts to meet some distorted idea of reality, and was headed toward a life of health, happiness, and honesty. And I will never forget my sponsor's reaction. With a quiet smile he said, "Welcome to the program," and gave me a bear hug so tight that I can still feel it in both my body and soul.

Every year, I do another round of Steps Four and Five, perhaps with an emphasis, one year, on my job, another on my family, the next revisiting my abysmal treatment of subordinates.

Step Six - *Were entirely ready to have God remove all these defects of character.*

Step Seven - *Humbly asked Him to remove our shortcomings.*

Ready, indeed! Thanks to Steps One, Two and Three, we've achieved and maintain sobriety. In Steps Four and Five we acknowledged our transgressions, saw just how screwed up we had become; for the first time in memory, we had come clean and made peace with ourselves. We're not really bad people but are people who have done some bad things, for which we need the forgiveness of God.

You might ask, what are "defects of character" or "shortcomings" that we want God to remove? I'm pretty sure you already know whatever baggage you may be carrying around, but should you need a refresher, you could start with the classic "Seven Deadly Sins"—wrath, greed, sloth, pride, lust, envy, and gluttony—and add dishonesty, procrastination, fear, cowardice, impatience, laziness, denial, guilt, resentment, self-pity, negative thinking, and anything else that might come to mind when you start making the list.

It is hard to describe to someone who doesn't have our disease, the really good feeling that we now have. We don't have to keep going back and beating ourselves up over what we have done in the past. But we've learned that we can't move forward, can't remove the great weight that has been pressing us down and holding us back, without the help of our higher power. Steps Six and Seven echo—no, call it "reinforce"— Step Three, and offer promise for the future. It's time for a fresh start!

Step Eight - *Made a list of all persons we had harmed, and became willing to make amends to them all.*

Step Nine - *Made direct amends to such people wherever possible, except when to do so would injure them or others.*

When you finish Steps Four and Five you are

hurting; you feel better after Six and Seven—
and then you are faced with the harsh reality
of Eight and Nine. To this point, you have
been working on yourself, and you have been
changing. Now, you literally step outside of the
program and have to deal with the minefield
of wreckage you have left behind you, the
havoc wrought on so many of your personal
relationships.

In Step Eight, you must make a list, very
specific and clear, of just how you have harmed
people. Written out, chapter and verse, what
you did to whom, when, how, why, and to what
specific effect. Note that, in Step Nine, you
will be required to make amends directly to
any or all of your victims who you can find and
indirectly to those who have died or disappeared.
Specificity is vital, because this will literally
provide the "talking points" you will need in
Step Nine. You start with the highest-priority
victim—yourself—then work your way down.
Yourself? Haven't you been serially damaged by
your own actions? You bet! Consider Step Eight
a summation of all steps that went before and a
punch-list for your own future.

Some people, new to the program, look over the list of Steps and want to jump right to Eight and Nine; they can see the benefits. However, unless they have been fully prepared in mind, body, and spirit by Steps One through Seven, jumping ahead will only be a temporary band-aid. You must learn to walk before you try to run.

Ideally, in Step Nine, you will sit down with each of your victims, everyone on the list, look them square in the eyes and not only offer an honest apology for what you have done and make amends to repair whatever was "broken," but make a firm commitment that it won't happen again. If appropriate, you will outline your plan to remedy the wrong; perhaps someone lost money because of your actions (or inaction), how do you intend to repay them? But overall, to regain their trust, you must do more: pledge a broader change; you are not only apologizing for the pain or humiliation you have brought to this one person, but you are admitting that there have been others and that you are adopting a whole new approach to life. You may or may not be forgiven but you must accept the outcome

My Step Eight list was pretty long and, in a word, sobering. I remembered things I had long forgotten (and at first, I wished they could have stayed that way). Right up front—after yours truly—was my family. As I began Step Nine, I first labored long and hard over letters to Kate and each of our kids, letters of apology, seeking forgiveness. I owed Kate more than I could ever put in a letter, but I tried. I know that my kids had suffered from my constant absence from home—even when I was not traveling, home was the place where I often ended up after the kids had gone to bed and when I was "home" I was often so angry that they didn't want to be around me—they suffered from being held to some of the same bullshit standards I had to deal with while growing up. (Being grounded, for example, because I came home "too late" after going to a Friday night high school football game with some friends . . . when my parents had no idea when the game had actually ended.)

One at a time, I handed each their letter, sat down and waited while they read them, then offered to discuss. My kids all responded, "Don't worry, you were a great dad." Yeah, maybe, but more likely their mother had raised them to be non-judgmental and kind. Nonetheless, from that day forward, I have tried to be the father I should have been for so many years. No, not "tried"—I have *been* their father, friend, mentor, and companion.

As I worked through my list, I sat down with everyone I could and sent detailed letters to those where a face-to-face was not practical. I found some victims who refused to talk with me; I sent them letters anyway, but did not further force myself upon them. Some indeed had died; I worked with my sponsors to find some method to meet my own commitment to make amends. Perhaps a contribution to their favorite charity, if that could be determined, or volunteering my time to an AA prison ministry.

Let me provide one significant, but difficult, personal story of contrition. There was a mid-level executive at our company, on the way up, for whom I developed an intense dislike. If I could have any negative influence on his career, I exercised it. I spread rumors, belittled his achievements, questioned (to senior management) his abilities. My efforts were not all that successful, but probably had some impact, some delay in a promotion.

My sponsor said, "It's time to make amends."

OK, if I was going to play this AA game (although, of course, it was deadly serious business) I would have to play by all of the rules. So I called my victim, who by then was working half-way across the country, "Hey, it's Tommy. I'm going to be in your town day after tomorrow, are you free for dinner?"

I flew out, checked into a hotel, he came by to meet me in the bar and we went in to dinner. Small talk, "whatever happened to?" sort of thing. I almost chickened out, several times. But I knew I had to do this, and finally said, "This is awkward, but there is something I have to tell you. I am a recovering alcoholic, I have been active in AA for some time and one of the most important steps in recovery is to admit to misdeeds, reach out and seek forgiveness."

"Gee, Tom, good for you, no big surprise, everyone knew you had a problem . . . "

"More than you know," I said. "In the past, I did everything I could to sabotage your career. I don't really know why, I simply didn't like you and did not want you to be successful."

If the phrase, "his jaw dropped," has any meaning, it surely applied here. And I pressed on: "And I need to ask for your forgiveness."

I would not have been surprised had he reacted in any reasonably predictable fashion: anger, throw something, storm out of the room. In truth, he didn't react much at all. Sort of, "Uh, well, yeah . . ." and our conversation was basically over. But I had done what I needed to do, and I know it took him some time to process his own feelings. Sometime later, he sent me a note, a kind note, thanking me for my honesty and giving me what I needed: forgiveness.

Step Ten - *Continued to take personal inventory and when we were wrong promptly admitted it.*

Step Eleven - *Sought through prayer and meditation to improve our conscious contact with God as we understood Him, praying only for knowledge of His will for us and the power to carry that out.*

Steps Ten and Eleven are like moving on to AA graduate school. We have learned the basics, and now put them into action. With Step Ten, we can take a daily personal inventory, play back the events of the day—relive, regret, and admit our mistakes, and move to make amends (as soon as feasible) before we pick up some more baggage and resentments have a chance to flourish. Every day, a fresh start.

As for Step Eleven—earlier, I described the morning and evening prayer routine that helped me focus, one day at a time. Let me emphasize: if we do something every day the act doesn't get exaggerated—nor do we.

Step Twelve - *Having had a spiritual awakening as the result of these steps, we tried to carry this message to alcoholics, and to practice these principles in all our affairs.*

Step Twelve urges us to get outside of ourselves and do something good for someone else, other addicts. By doing so, we help ourselves as well. In truth, as a corollary, I have heard that sponsors often get more benefit from their efforts than do the people they sponsor.

Thus, for Step Twelve, you must find your voice. Not to talk to yourself, I'm sure you have plenty of opportunities to do just that—but to reach out, use your voice, the expression of what you have learned about yourself, your disease, to guide other users through the swamp.

May I suggest, move outside of your comfort zone? For many years, I held meetings at a local hospital where the street people, the homeless, would end up for treatment. More than once, I was asked by well-meaning friends, "Why do you bother with them? They're not open to your help, they'll just be cycling in and out of the hospital."

My friends were correct. The patients would be dredged out of the gutter by the cops, dumped in the hospital, dried out, turned out, and soon enough were back in the gutter and then in the hospital. Indeed, why bother?

Because they need to know that there will always be somebody there to open the door through which they may, eventually, walk. Back when I was just getting fully into recovery, I know how important it was for me, every time I walked into a meeting, to know that there was someone who cared about me.

This book is part of my own Step Twelve commitment. I have walked in your shoes, I know how bad it can be, and I know how much AA has helped me. I want you to try, go to a meeting, ask some questions. You don't have to sign a pledge, you just have to be willing to listen. □

MY STORY ... AND OTHERS

Being open and honest in how you handle your sobriety is always a difficult thing. There are federal laws that protect you, alcoholism is a disease and you don't really have to tell anyone. But, if you're serious about getting ahead of the problem, wouldn't you want to have more people on your side? When I told my boss—who happened to be the chairman of the company—that I was in the program, he was surprised, because my addictions were fed after work, I was careful when in business/social settings, and I don't know if he ever saw me drunk. But he was very kind. "Good for you!" he said, and added, "Tom, you are one of my most valued associates. If you ever need to change something, perhaps not travel so much, whatever, let me know I will be totally supportive."

I appreciated his concern, but I didn't want any special consideration. Knowing that he trusted me was enough, and you can bet that this gave me an extra incentive to stay clean. I also became the go-to guy when a senior executive seemed to be having, well, a problem. I would get a call from the chairman or the Human Resources VP: might I have a conversation with "Joe X"? Far better, I think, than having Joe X called on the carpet and interrogated, however sensitively it may have been handled, by someone in HR.

I would sit down and tell Joe X my story and offer some suggestions; perhaps he might start by getting some advice from the Employee Assistance Program. I think one or two might have taken that advice, but for the most part, these were people who believed that they had too much to lose if word got around, and I suspect they didn't trust anyone to keep their secret. One guy said, "Look, if the boss knew I had a drinking problem, he wouldn't trust me to deal with anything important." I suggested that the boss probably already knew, and would welcome his honesty and pledge of an effort to stop or control the behavior. "I'm living proof," I said.

Over time, I believe I was helpful in getting a dozen good men and women into the program, and to this day, many years later, I'm included in the anniversary celebrations of many.

Not every effort panned out. Some results were neutral . . . drinking was cut back, but not enough and posed some problems along the way. There were two heart wrenching disasters, two guys with no insight who made no effort. Both were fighter pilots: one was a former member of the USAF Thunderbirds flight demonstration team, the other had been in the Rhodesian Air Force.

The ex-Thunderbird lived up to the popular image of a fighter pilot as a hard living, hard drinking hero. I think he actually believed that stuff. We put him through three rehab programs, without a scintilla of success. The Rhodesian became an American citizen and was one of our international marketing experts, but couldn't handle being away from his family so much of the time. Both of these wonderful men were killed by their disease.

Let me add a small but telling postscript. In 1990, perhaps ten years after having revealed my disease to the boss, I was appointed president of a major unit of our company. It was headquartered in Phoenix, and I was pretty up-tight. I'd heard that Arizona folks were very conservative, socially and politically, and I certainly didn't know how the employees might react if they knew that their new boss was an alcoholic. So the first night I was in town, ready to report to work the next morning, I really wanted a meeting, found one, and attended. Maybe a dozen people, offering the same loving support I found at any meeting. I spoke briefly, introduced myself as new in town but didn't elaborate.

The next day, my first day on the job (but not my first visit to that plant. I knew my way around). Bright and early, before the work day began, I parked in my assigned space right outside the door and started through the cafeteria, toward the elevators. Over at one side was a small group of men listening to an older fellow who, from his dress—no suit or tie—clearly was not an executive, but from his manner was probably some sort of team leader. He looked familiar but I couldn't place him; however, as soon as he saw me, he said, with great enthusiasm, "Hey, there's the guy I was telling you about! Hey, Tom, come over here." So I did, and he said to his group, "Folks, this is Tom G, our new friend, I met him at my AA meeting last night. He's really a good guy." I didn't know what to say except, good morning, nice meeting you, shook a few hands and escaped to the elevator.

I'm sure the news went through all 10,000 employees within a nanosecond. I don't recall any repercussions, but it just proves the value of being up-front and out in front. Ah, but you may say, had I not gone to the meeting, if I was not a member of AA, no one would have been the wiser. Ah, I would say, I'd rather be identified as someone who was working on his problem, than as a falling-down drunk spotted in a local tavern.

Here's a related story. Before my wife moved out to join me in Arizona, I would commute back home on the weekends. During the week, I was wrestling with serious problems at the plant, it had been losing money, there were too many employees, I really needed the support of a regular meeting. I looked in the "Where and When" (you know, before the internet) book, a guide to meetings (place, type, program). Well, I spotted a meeting near my hotel but didn't bother with the "description," any meeting would suit me. I pulled into the parking lot and parked next to a motorcycle, went in and sat down. There was at that point only one other attendee, clearly the motorcycle driver—easily spotted by his bandana and tattoos covering the visible surface of his body. Very gruff guy. He asked me what was I doing there? And I said, I'm here for the AA meeting. He said, "Oh?"

During that brief conversation, three or four more guys came in, all members of the motorcycle fraternity, looking at me kinda funny. Finally, my friend said, "I'm chairing the meeting tonight. Have you been in the program very long?" Yeah, quite a few years. "Well," he said, "this is a gay biker's meeting." So I looked him in the eye and said, "I don't care, I need a meeting and I'm staying."

I actually attended this meeting regularly for maybe the next seven months. They were very kind to me, and they would tease me about being straight. They never made me feel uncomfortable, but they brought a lot of good messages, about openness, about our disease—

an equal opportunity destroyer. Race, sex, ethnic background, sexual preferences, didn't make any difference. Other than some tales of the home life, our stories were all the same.

I've always had a sponsor, sometimes multiple sponsors (it has not been unusual for me to have as many as five at the same time, although I should point out that one sponsor is the norm and that many people in AA frown on having multiple-sponsors; I only know, it works for me). In truth, when I am asked to be a sponsor, I always counter, "Only if you will also be my sponsor." I believe this co-sponsorship arrangement helps both people, helps establish trust. You can have any sort of arrangement with which you would be comfortable. Or no arrangement at all. There are no fixed rules.

I noted, above, that your sponsor is not "your new best friend." But that's a generic, not specific, caution. It doesn't mean that you can't be close friends with a sponsor. One of my sponsors is a Jesuit priest with whom I have dinner once a week, just the two of us, going back many years. We share long-term sobriety. And a friendship.

As a sponsor myself, I had no problem when dealing with issues of the disease itself, but I would sometimes come up against challenges of day-to-day living that I was not really equipped, by training or experience, to handle. I sponsored a young man who was a policeman and was having problems with some part of his training. I asked a friend from AA, who was also in law enforcement, to step in and help. I sponsored a physician who needed advice on issues more properly provided by another doctor.

I have sponsored women—gay and straight—and along the way gained valuable insight into what are some special gender issues. Back when I was "in treatment," one of the therapists, herself a woman in recovery, discussed the impact of alcoholism on women. While there are many similarities (the destruction of clear thinking, of responsible actions, and of honesty) there are some differences—physiological, as noted earlier, and cultural (or gender-specific) things you might not think about. One simple example: a single woman with children (or a married woman with a working husband) might have trouble finding child support to cover a twenty-eight day in-house treatment program.

Those women I have sponsored each brought a fresh perspective to our disease. Recurring themes, as you might expect, have been early sexual abuse by relatives and continuing domestic violence at the hands of an alcoholic spouse. One of my long-running confidants, call her "Maxine," acknowledged that using alcohol increased chances of being a victim . . . but, also, increased the chance that the drinker would become a perpetrator. Once she entered recovery—after years of denial—Maxine was devastated to realize that she had been visiting destructive behavior on her own children, passing along things that had happened to her as if she had been in training to be a bad mother.

Maxine's journey of recovery began with an enlightened employee assistance program and continues through active membership in AA, which she embraces as her "safe haven." AA allows her to reveal bad actions and articulate hidden feelings in the comfort of an understanding group. As she told me, she left every meeting feeling "cleansed and redeemed."

I would note that, as a sponsor of women, I was never comfortable when it came to relationship issues and in all such cases I invited someone more qualified to step in, while I continued to help with the disease.

I should note, also, another type of special case: call it, dual-diagnosis, alcoholism and, say, schizophrenia or bi-polar disease, where treatment is more complicated; a team approach might work best involving medical professionals along with attendance at AA meetings and work with sponsors.

It's not uncommon for people to fool around with the program for a while before they "get it." While in the test drive (or it could be the "get the spouse off my back") mode, they do not necessarily tell the truth. You don't want to be judgmental (there but for the grace of God . . .) but you don't want to let them get away with obvious evasions. For things that are not so obvious, you want to fine-tune your bullshit meter.

Here's one example. I'm a big fisherman. Often, I would invite someone I was sponsoring to go fishing with me, a relaxed setting that encouraged openness. One of my "guests" was a middle-aged guy with a houseful of kids who owned a neighborhood bar. He had been going to daily meetings for some time, and in all of our one-on-one conversations he assured me that was doing "Fine" and was diligently working through the little exercises I had assigned. Well, I've always thought that "Fine" could be a codeword for something less than "fine," and after one meeting where he seemed more than usually troubled. I said, "Let's go fishing." I don't think he was much for fishing—not since he was a kid, anyway, hunting bluegills on a worm-baited safety pin—but he said, "OK why not?"

I took him out on a beautiful day. We were both catching fish and I think he was actually having fun. But he clearly wanted to talk, and after a few bumbling attempts ("Uh . . . ah . . . oh, I—") he said that he lied at the meetings, about anything and everything, and the only time he told me the truth was when he said, "I'd like to have you as my sponsor." The only time he was sober, he admitted, was during the meetings. After which he would go to his bar, go upstairs to the office to "do the books" and drink.

He realized that he couldn't stop drinking, but wanted to.

I said, "Let's work on the main trigger here,

the bar." I told him to call me every day for the next month just when he arrived at the office. "If I'm not available," I instructed, "leave a message, I will get back to you as soon as possible." Thus, even if he didn't speak to me immediately, he was telling me that he had not yet had a drink that day and he would be focused on waiting for my call. He lived about a block from his church, so I also suggested that he stop in at church every day, say a prayer, ask for strength. This gave him something to do, something for which he could hold himself accountable.

He's now been clean for more than 15 years.

I became the sponsor for a man who had been so high and fallen so low. A successful businessman, president of the company for which he worked, until booze took over his life—multi-martini lunches followed by series of chasers from a bottle of gin in his bottom desk drawer. He spent his afternoons yelling at his staff. He was, of course, very sophisticated so at home at dinner he switched to wine and spent his evenings yelling at his wife and kids. It didn't take long until he was thrown out of the company and his life became a total mess.

He had not yet been thrown out of the house, but as you will imagine, he was having a lot of trouble at home. I told him: write a very detailed letter to your wife, and the same to each of the kids. Explain why you have been acting badly— no excuses, none of the "I was drinking because" BS. Accept responsibility and ask for forgiveness for each hurtful thing you have done. Bring the letters to me, and then we can decide if you should actually send them.

He put in great effort, taking almost a month to write and edit and re-write, and he really laid everything on the line, even to confessing to things that no one knew about. The letters were absolutely beautiful, descriptive, poignant. So then I said, it's now up to you. You can send the letters . . . or, since you are so thoroughly prepared, why not just sit down with each member of your family and tell them in person? And so he did. He told me how hard it was, but how meaningful.

He never got his old job back, but his investment portfolio was solid and he has been able to convert his work experience into a consulting business that helps struggling small businesses for a very modest fee.

The role of "sponsor" can take many different forms. Once, I took over as sponsor for a young man who had been in the program for a couple of years—he was about twenty-five, half my age at the time, working at some menial job with no real future. I asked him, what did he want to do with his life and he said, "From the time I was five years old and got a fireman's helmet for Christmas, I knew that I was going to be a fireman when I grew up. But . . ." he paused, and then added, "they require a high school diploma and I don't have one."

Twenty-five years old and no diploma? This was, in this day and age, for an obviously intelligent, motivated guy, a real anomaly. So I asked . . . how come?

"Well, I was the last child in a pretty large family, and all of my brothers and sisters were put through top-notch Catholic schools . . . but in my senior year in high school, my father was laid off from his job and was not able to pay the tuition for the last semester."

"So?"

"So the school refused to give me a diploma."

I was shocked. I knew the school, couldn't imagine such behavior, so I called, made an appointment with the principal, and told him the story: this kid had completed all of his classes, earned his diploma but the school refused to award it because of unpaid tuition. He looked up the file, said, "That's right. No tuition, no diploma. We have a 'no tolerance' policy."

"Not even for a family that was on the verge of bankruptcy?"

"Zero tolerance means zero tolerance."

I was so outraged that, truth to tell, I wanted to punch him in his smug smiling face. But, truth to tell, I had been working for years on "anger management" and came forth with a better solution. "How much," I asked, "does he owe?"

I pulled out my checkbook, wrote a check, thrust it at the principal and asked, "When may I pick up his diploma?"

Startled into temporary incoherence, he finally stammered, "Tomorrow, tomorrow would be fine."

Sure, but not fine with me. Yes, I picked it up, and passed it on to the young man. But I wasn't about to let the school get away with such perversity. Whatever happened, I wondered, to the idea that you don't visit the sins of the fathers on the sons? (If, indeed, losing a job was a "sin.") Or whatever happened to simple, basic, Christian compassion? So I called on someone higher in the administrative chain, who was as appalled as I. And the policy was changed on the spot, and remains so to this day. Did I get my money back? No, I didn't want my money back. I took up this cause on the merits, not on my financial involvement. My "investment" got my crusading foot in the door and, I hope, created opportunities for other students, then and in the future.

I presented the diploma as a gift to the young man, but there seemed to be a glitch. He called and said, "I have a problem, I have the application in front of me and they ask, have you ever used drugs?"

I said, "Why is this hard? You've been clean for a long time."

He said, "I really want this, but now I'm afraid."

"Well," I said, "you have a disease, but you're protected under the law. They can't discriminate as long as you are truthful." You need to explain, I explained—been sober for maybe two years, you are a new you. So he put it in the application, and was accepted for training. He has been very successful, promoted several times, and I still see him every once in a while at meetings.

But—what's really interesting about this story . . . after he had been in the AA program a couple of years, he told me he'd fallen in love, the girl of his dreams, and they were going to be married. I said, "Great!" But he said, "There's something I haven't told you, I've never told anyone. I have another problem: I'm not drinking, but I think I'm a sex addict."

"Huh? You're kidding me! You hang out in bars, not drinking, but looking for a hook-up?"

"No," he said, "I'm addicted to pornography and masturbation—a big problem, this has taken over, has control of me, I want to do this more than to actually make love, every night, and I don't know how I'm going to deal with this when I'm married. I have visions, telling my bride 'I have a headache' and after she's asleep, going to the computer and searching for naked celebrities."

I put him in touch with a PhD psychologist who was a specialist in this area; he provided some counsel and got him into a special "sex addicts anonymous" program, modeled on the AA Twelve Step program. The group had meetings, Wednesdays at noon, at the same club and just down the hall from the room where we had our "home" AA meetings. It worked: today, totally over the sex issue, he goes to AA meetings and doesn't need the other.

Sometimes, we live in a pretty small world. One Wednesday, not long after my fireman friend had "graduated" from the SA program, I was at the club for lunch—scheduled to meet with a young man I had agreed to sponsor, so we could go over some ground rules. I was early, and just hanging around, when a man I knew from church came over. We had been acquaintances for some time, his kids went to school with my kids and once he had asked me for a favor, he was up for a pretty good job and wondered if I might put in a good word. I did, and he got the job, and now, here he was, and I'd never seen him around the club before. So I asked him, what's up?

"Oh," he said, "I'm going to a meeting . . ." And it hit me right away, noon on Wednesday, it was the meeting for sex addicts! I said good for you, great, how are you doing, he said, "I've never done it before, heard about it, read about it, and want to try it." But he also said, "I'm really scared. I came by here last week but couldn't find the courage to go upstairs." I said, this is a very safe place, and I'll take you up and introduce you to the chair, and we did that, and I went back downstairs for my own lunch meeting. Later, my church-friend called to give me a report. The meeting was good, he was definitely going to continue. He said he felt comfortable asking me for help and wondered if perhaps we could get together once in a while? Would I be his sponsor? I asked if he had any issues with alcohol or drugs and he said "No. My issue purely sex." Now, this was not my area of experience or expertise, but I certainly understood the process.

It turned out that he had been physically abused by an uncle at a very early age, and it really screwed him up. Over the years, he had seen a series of therapists who had been of some help but he was carrying a huge burden, a burning resentment and a truck-load of shame which he couldn't unload. I gave him a simple assignment: for each of the next twenty-eight days, you must pray for your uncle—ask God to find him and help him to heal. And every day you must forgive your uncle, and forgive yourself.

Just a month later, I got a surprise delivery at home, a very good bottle of wine and a note: "I have finished the twenty-eight days. I am feeling much better, and by way of thanks I wanted to give you something symbolic. I hope you wife enjoys the wine!" And so she did.

I saw him a few more times, but he was well on his way to healing. "Your twenty-eight day sentence really worked," he admitted. "I had been trying to forget the past, you made me confront it . . . and it doesn't hurt anymore." □

LESSONS LEARNED . . . AND SHARED

I directly attribute much of my success to lessons learned in AA. By my "first birthday" celebration, I knew that I would never be healthy enough to walk away from AA. That I was trapped in a life-long struggle, that I would always be "recovering," never recovered.

I wish everyone, not just addicts, could go through a 28 day program and then attend meetings—you learn so much about the fundamentals of living, about honesty, about accepting others no matter how different their backgrounds and interests.

Here are a few thoughts . . .

☐ Be honest and open from the very beginning of any relationship. It is almost impossible to go back and rebuild trust that you have lost. People of good will, will (usually) forget and forgive what you say to them, people will (usually) forget and forgive what you do to them but people will never forget and rarely forgive how you make them feel about themselves. As in, at a staff meeting, as I so often have done, singling out someone who has made an error and yelling.

☐ Pay your debts—and I don't mean just those involving money. If you owe someone an acknowledgment, or a favor to be returned, or an apology for a slight or oversight, pay it. Keep a running mental score card.

☐ Learn to "let go." I wasn't an angry young man—but I was a very angry adult. I harbored grudges, nursed what I assumed to be slights, and let resentments roil around inside my soul. I would get angry at somebody and keep that anger for years . . . then, more than once and much to my surprise and embarrassment, I would run into one of those targets and discover how nice they were and then couldn't remember why I disliked them so much in the first place. Well, I'm long out of the "resentment" business, I'm 66 years

old and there is not enough time left to
clear out any new anger.

If you've read this far—and still are wavering,
uncertain, let me offer one final thought. I always
was good at my job in spite of the fact that I
was using. After I came clean, I was *very* good at
my job. I always thought that booze made me super
creative, helping me write all of those speeches and
position papers and marketing plans, and I was on
top of the world! Truth was, I was very good at fak-
ing it. Call it style over substance. Not until I got
sober did I learn how creative I *really* could be. □

EPILOG

Before I found AA, I did not know how to live a sober life and my emotional development was frozen in my early teens. I know in my heart that AA saved my life and let me become the person I was meant to be—the person I wanted to be. The Program gave me control of my life—a gift I share with millions of others. Yes, we know that not everyone who enters the program will stay with the program; many drop out, but some of those will later give it another try and find that it does, indeed, "work."

We're raised to believe that by being strong, we can do anything. Well, maybe, sometimes. If you have our disease, you can't stop drinking anymore than you can wish away cancer. The paradox of AA is that you have to surrender, to admit failure, before you can win.

Come. Walk this path with me. In your new life, your worst day will be better than the best day, drunk.   ■